Grandma,

Merry Christmas!,
Sending you unconditional Love
and lots of Hugs. Best
wishes for a Job Killed 2006.

Love,

Eric, Megan,
Melra, & Portia

Unconditional
LOVE

Unconditional LOVE

VOLUME ONE

Understanding the Psychology and Embodied Daily Life Practice of Unconditional Love

by
Eric Bonnici

Published by Luminary Media Group,
an imprint of Pine Orchard, Inc.
www.pineorchard.com

Information and availability:
www.4Totale.com

First Printing: Autumn 2005
Printed in Canada

ISBN 1-930580-91-6
EAN 9781930580916
Library of Congress Control Number 2005934237

Printed with soy ink on recycled paper
100% post-consumer fiber
totally treated without chlorine

*This book is dedicated
to Unconditional Love—the most
profound inspiration and guidance
for sharing my understanding
of Unconditional Love
to the world.*

If we are concerned about the world in which we live and want to make a difference, we only need to be willing to face the humility and dignity of who we really are. Life will always present us with experiences, individually and globally, that continually move us toward facing the precious qualities that lie within each of us. It is only when we are willing to find the balance between humility and dignity that we begin to understand and truly enjoy what this journey of life and death has to offer.

—Eric Bonnici

Contents

PART II
The Embodied Daily Life Practice
of Unconditional Love

Acknowledgements

Iwould like to acknowledge and thank all those who have supported me on my journey of writing this book and who have constantly encouraged me to bring it to life:

My mother for always believing in me; my father as my original teacher and mentor; my brother, who has been a great support and coach; my wife, who is an inspiration with all she has already achieved in her life, for all her feedback, and her willingness to share the journey from the day we met; and to my grandmother, for her amazing courage and faith.

Thank you to my friends, Jim Mori and Katie Minkus, and to my family, for helping me refine and edit my message and for their invaluable input and support.

Thank you to my principal editor and friend, Katie Callender, as well as to Matt and Carolyn from Pine Orchard, who have helped in designing and putting this book together for print.

And thank you to the friends and family who have given me the pictures to help convey the reality of Unconditional Love.

Foreword

My name is Andrew Shugyo Bonnici and I am a Doctor of Psychology, a Buddhist priest, a Zen teacher, a published author, artist, and a worldwide counselor in Applied Meditation Therapy. It is a privilege and an honor to be writing the foreword for this book written by my son, Eric. I am proud to be his father, but I am also blessed to be his mentor, his original Zen teacher, the spiritual sealer of his marriage, and his lifelong friend in the Way.

From the very beginning of his life, throughout his formative years, and now as a man, a husband, and a father, Eric has always demonstrated a depth of heart, sincerity, compassion, and spirituality that can call out the best in others. Over the last ten years, I have watched Eric follow his inner calling to actualize a vision and a dream of world peace and loving kindness based on the acceptance of our fears. This vision of hope is based on Eric's daily commitment to practice the heart of Unconditional Love and to embrace the common human experience of primordial fear. Over the years, he has worked hard to conceptually refine the clarity of his vision and the communication of its practical application to everyday life and relationships. Although this book is the culmination of many years of inner work and writing, it also represents Eric's ongoing commitment to meditation life practice, psychological studies, personal somatic research, interpersonal growth, and the spiritual refinement of his body, speech, heart, and mind.

As Eric moved toward the embodied actualization and communication of his vision, he had to make difficult choices and change his life in many ways. He listened to his inner calling and trusted it to guide him toward the actualization of his vision in his own life and in the life of others. He trusted the meaning and the guidance of his spiritual integrity, even though it caused emotional pain, anxiety, and fear to himself and sometimes to those around him. It takes courage to accept our primordial fear and live from Unconditional Love in a world that is conditioned by the illusions of differences, exclusions, and separateness.

In this book, Eric shares his understanding of our common primordial fear and how the misunderstanding of it prevents us from living a life of unconditional love, embodied truth, joyful compassion, relational wisdom, and world peace. He shares the basis of primordial fear as the original fear of meeting, accepting, and being the Unconditional Self. It is primordial fear that assures us of our Unconditional Nature. It is through understanding and embracing this primordial fear that we can understand, embrace, and live in Unconditional Love. His sharing and his teachings cover the physical, psychological, emotional, spiritual, and practical application of living from Unconditional Love. He shares his practice of living this vision with very concrete experiential skills and behavioral forms that can be readily applied in everyday life.

I respect the evolutionary human potential of his vision. I honor the work and the courage it took to bring this vision and his teaching of Unconditional Love to a world of human beings kept apart by illusory conditions. It is a realistic and achievable vision that, if followed and practiced, can bring healing and peace to you, to your loved ones, to your communities, and to the world as a whole.

This book is only the inspirational beginning. It is a calling for you to have the dedication and the courage to practice living from love rather than from your personal fears. It is a calling to embrace the felt truth of our common primordial fear and to practice our daily life from the heart of Unconditional Love. It is a calling to passionately affirm and actualize the radical vision of ourselves and our world at peace. I encourage you to embody

Eric's vision, to practice it in your daily life, and to share this vision of living Unconditional Love with others.

With blessing and encouragement,
—Dr. Andrew Shugyo Bonnici
July 12, 2005

The more we, as humans,
accept how we experience
Unconditional Love in our
day-to-day life, the closer
we come to realizing
peace on
earth.

—Eric Bonnici

Introduction

My journey writing about Unconditional Love sprang from a vision I received during a sitting, practicing one of the techniques you will learn in this book. The vision was to share Unconditional Love with the world.

When I stood up from this sitting, I began to see more of life than I had ever seen before. I had always seen Unconditional Love in everyone and everything, but after my vision, what I began to see differently was that Unconditional Love was not seen by everyone around me. I started noticing the layers inside myself and others that seem to keep Unconditional Love hidden and separate.

The task of sharing Unconditional Love with the world seemed mammoth. It terrified and overwhelmed me. Yes, I was overwhelmed with the idea of writing, of tackling such a project, as writing was never one of my specialties, but I was more overwhelmed by the changes occurring within me.

*Unconditional Love is all
around; the only way to see
it is to reflect it from within.*

*It is in the continued practice
of accepting our own fear
that we reveal our unconditional
nature from within.*

I felt at peace with my new knowing because it came to me so profoundly. However, as a conditioned human (which you will learn more about later), I had to grapple with the idea that here I was, a man, involved in sports, my traditional work, and family, facing this intense calling to teach about Unconditional Love.

I had to get past my conditioned illusions that "love," or talking about any kind of love, is a feminine thing. I had to trust my vision, accept my fear, and absolutely change my life.

This meant picking up and moving geographically, thus separating myself from my defined identity at that time. It was not a cut-all-ties kind of separation. I still maintained the emotional bond with my family via frequent communication and visits. My move was more a separation I needed to distinguish myself as myself and to relieve myself of the daily distractions of my former life in order to focus on my new task at hand. I needed the space to welcome in my calling.

It is absolutely possible to understand all human experience unconditionally, and that is through one's own body.

What I realized in welcoming my calling is that, as human beings, we have a multitude of ways to express how we feel inside. These different forms of expression have separated us because no one human being can mentally understand the myriad expressions of all human kind. One might be a world traveler, a scholar of many languages and cultures, yet due to the limitations of one's conditional life, even a lifetime of travel and study would only begin to scratch the surface of cognitively understanding all human experience.

However, it is absolutely possible to understand all human experience unconditionally, and that is through one's own body. If we look at what is physiologically going on inside the human body that creates different ways of expression, we have a chance of truly understanding our fellow humans.

The chapters that follow will unravel the mystery of understanding through Unconditional Love. This book defines the psychology and physiology behind emotions expressed

Create the world we deserve,
living as an unconditional being in a
world of conditions.

from the experience of Unconditional Love, and will give you tools and techniques to better physically understand and experience Unconditional Love in everyday life.

Such practice will also deepen your relationships with yourself and others and will eventually help clarify your purpose in being exactly who you are right now and your continued evolution. The practice will ultimately show that you are doing everything needed to create the world we deserve, by living as an unconditional being in a world of conditions.

Understanding the Psychology of Unconditional Love

Individual Truths and Universal Truths

There are many truths in the world. Some are individual or relative truths, and others are universal truths. Relative truths are experienced individually; universal truths are experienced by all human beings.

Whether something is a universal truth or a relative truth can be revealed through the question: "How many different examples are there of this truth?"

If it is true for only one, then it is an individual or relative truth. Likewise, if a truth includes many people yet leaves out just one human being, it is a relative truth. We can see many examples of this relative truth all around us because human beings accept life in many ways.

A universal truth always grows to include any new experience or knowledge that has been acquired through all life experience. The need

A universal truth is seen in everything from the smallest to the largest known living thing.

for love and the condition of fear are universal truths. Our ongoing experiences of change, illness, old age, and death are also examples of universal truths. A universal truth is seen in everything from the smallest to the largest known living thing.

Part of this world's beauty is our individuality and diversity.

Individuality and Diversity

Part of this world's beauty is our individuality and diversity. However, the individuality and diversity of relative truths can be a little scary for those who may not understand or accept the way someone else describes his or her experience. As humans, we become overwhelmed thinking about the multitude of ways to describe an experience, so we tend to stick with the one we believe maintains our individuality.

Although we want to be individuals, we also need to feel connected to others. Universal truths allow us to feel connected and still experience the diversity and individuality of human expression.

Love is acceptance.

*Love is also knowing
and understanding.*

Love

L ove can be described by using the word "acceptance." This is a physical state within the body, a pleasant experience of wonder, excitement, and inspiration.

One begins to sense a quality of emotional fulfillment and ease in the body when loved or accepted unconditionally. Conditioned love means you will accept someone or have these good feelings in your body about someone if certain conditions apply. And being "in love" is when we choose to practice these good feelings in the body toward someone or something.

Love can come from many things, such as a person, a place, an animal, or from inside ourselves. If we do not know something, we can try to understand it with our whole being; and if we can truly understand something with our whole being, we can accept it or embrace it with love. Thus, love is also knowing and understanding.

Sometimes you can accept, know, or love someone's individual essence immediately, but it takes a lifetime of practice to accept or love someone's total humanity.

Practice loving yourself. This is "good." Practice loving yourself and one other. This is "great." Practice loving yourself, another, everyone else and all of creation. This is "divine."

Sometimes you can accept, know, or love someone's individual essence immediately, but it takes a lifetime of practice to accept or love someone's total humanity. This is not only due to the depth of our individual essence or the conditional patterns of our personality, but it is also because we all have the potential to change and grow.

I remember meeting my wife for the first time and immediately seeing her individual essence and feeling her seeing my individual essence with no inhibitions or conditions between us. It is the daily practice of helping each other accept our ongoing human condition that allows us to continue clearly seeing each other's essence throughout our lifetime together.

If you choose to practice extending the depth of love or acceptance with yourself, this is "good." If you choose to do this with yourself and one other, this is "great." If you choose to do this with yourself, another, everyone else, and all of creation, this is "divine."

Unconditional Love

Total & Complete Acceptance

Total & Complete Knowing

Total & Complete Understanding

Wisdom That Penetrates
Both Life and Death

Unconditional Love

O nce we see "love" as a practice of acceptance, we can explore the deepest quality
of love known as "Unconditional Love." The
word "unconditional" means total or complete,
and "love" can mean accepting, understanding or knowing something. I put these two
words together in two ways. First, the type of
love that is "unconditional love" means total
or complete acceptance, total or complete
understanding, and total or complete knowing.
Second, "Unconditional Love" (capitalized)
takes "unconditional love" a step further and
can be described as an even deeper love; a vast
wisdom that penetrates life and death and that
is the wholeness and integrity of all creation.

We can find individual and collective
examples reminding us of unconditional love:
a man, a woman, a baby, an animal, nature, or
something greater. Different upbringings, cultures, or simply anything to which we relate,

*We are all talking about the same
thing, just describing it
in different ways.*

all create diverse such examples. However, the example, be it a person, symbol, act, or name, is only a conditional reminder of not only unconditional love but perhaps also of the greater Unconditional Love.

Considering the multitude of individual and collective examples of a greater Unconditional Love allows us to appreciate how similar we are. We are actually all talking about the same thing, just describing it in different ways.

*When we understand
Primordial Fear as a call to
our relationship with
Unconditional Love,
we minimize the root of all fears
in the world through the deepest
understanding of fear.*

Primordial Fear

Primordial Fear is a primitive, fundamental, and original fear created by the
relationship of opposites. These opposites are
any conditional existence in contrast to the
universal infinite presence of Unconditional
Love.

Wherever and whenever these opposites
come in contact with each other, a friction
arises. For human conditional beings, friction
arises because we are overwhelmed by and
fearful of the incomprehensible magnitude of all
the accepted information that is Unconditional
Love. This friction is a Primordial Fear that is
at one of the deepest levels of our unconscious
mind and is the underlying Fear of all other
fears.

Primordial Fear is the way that Unconditional Love relates to and communicates with
conditional beings in a conditional world, and
this is often misunderstood.

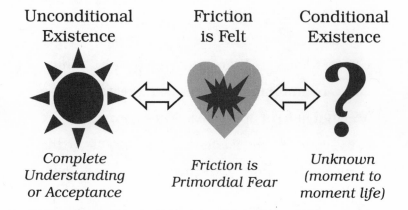

Unconditional Existence — Complete Understanding or Acceptance

Friction is Felt — Friction is Primordial Fear

Conditional Existence — Unknown (moment to moment life)

When we accept the call to this Primordial relationship with Unconditional Love, we begin to release our innate potential toward an infinite future of ever deepening growth, wisdom, compassion and understanding.

As conditional beings, we tend to label any felt bodily experience of fear in a negative way. But if we understand Primordial Fear as a call to our relationship with Unconditional Love, we minimize the root of all fears in the world through the deepest understanding of fear.

When we accept the call to this Primordial relationship with Unconditional Love, we begin to release our innate potential toward an infinite future of ever deepening growth, wisdom, compassion, and understanding.

A Primordial Fear can be felt as any experience where there is an energy shift or sensation happening in the body. When these energy shifts or sensations happen in our body, we label them "good" or "bad." Although we label them "good" or "bad," they are still the felt friction of Primordial Fear being physically released or held in the body. We have come up with many names for how we experience this felt friction depending on our upbringing, social context, and personal choices.

When we allow ourselves to feel the friction of Primordial Fear without labeling it as "good" or "bad" we can transform that felt friction into a more productive, enjoyable and creative way of life.

When we accept the felt friction of Primordial Fear, we may call it joy, wonder, happiness, excitement, inspiration, etc. These are feelings that are associated with allowing the felt friction to move freely through the body and be released.

For example, while waiting for my first child to be born, I experienced all of the above emotions. I was elated, ecstatic about meeting this little person, and felt I loved her intensely already. This was acceptance. However, along with the excitement came fear: Would I provide adequately for my family? Would I be a good father? This was my resistance.

When we resist or do not accept the felt friction of Primordial Fear, we might call it nervousness, anxiety, hesitation, fear, anger, hate, etc. These feelings are associated with holding the felt friction in the body, not allowing it to be released.

When we can accept the felt friction of Primordial Fear, we open ourselves to certain feelings arising in the body. Likewise, when

Acceptance and Resistance can become Inspiration and Passion.

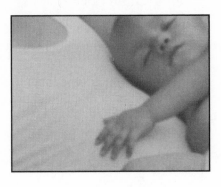

we fear or do not accept the felt friction of Primordial Fear, we resist opening ourselves to our immediate experience, generating other feelings in the body. This is not to say one is "good" or "bad." Rather it is to understand how we relate to the felt friction of Primordial Fear with acceptance or resistance.

When we allow ourselves to feel the friction of Primordial Fear without labeling it as "good" or "bad," we can transform that felt friction into a more productive, enjoyable, and creative way of life.

Through my experience of acceptance and resistance during the year my daughter was born and by practicing the techniques outlined in this book, I was able to double our business, build a house, and gain the confidence in knowing I would be the best father I could be. I was able to continue moving toward my excitement and fear through understanding my relationship with Unconditional Love. This is an example of the positive outcome of balancing both the acceptance and resistance with inspiration and passion.

*Understanding where the felt
friction of Primordial Fear arises
in the body gives us a chance to
experience our relationship with
Unconditional Love
in every day life.*

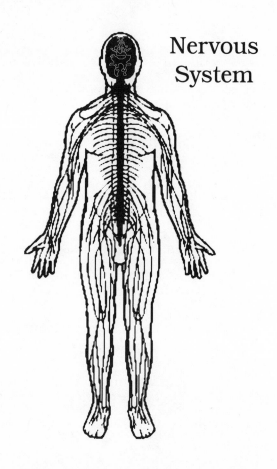

Nervous
System

Psychoneuroquantum Theory

Once we appreciate the nature of Primordial Fear, we can look at how and where this felt friction originates in the human body.

The origin of Primordial Fear in the human body is based on a quantum model of Nervous System Function developed by Andrew Shugyo Bonnici, Ph.D., in 1978. Because our nervous system is the neurobiological means by which we experience life, understanding how the felt friction of Primordial Fear arises through it gives us the chance to experience our relationship with Unconditional Love in everyday life. The following is a brief description of Dr. Bonnici's model:

Our brain and nervous system are the vehicles through which we experience life. The brain is the location where the neuro-circuitry of our personality and life experiences are

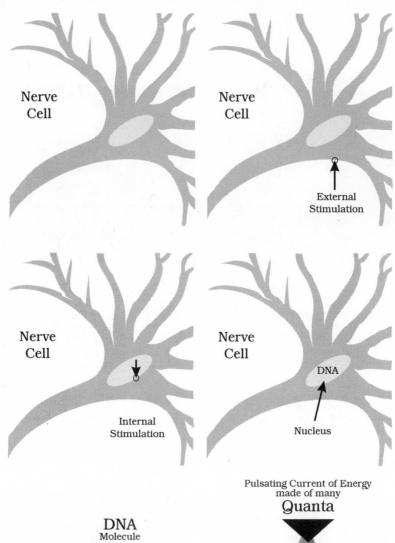

Nerve
Cell

Nerve
Cell

External
Stimulation

Nerve
Cell

Internal
Stimulation

Nerve
Cell

DNA

Nucleus

Pulsating Current of Energy
made of many
Quanta

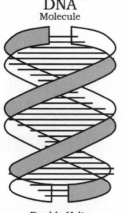

DNA
Molecule

Double Helix

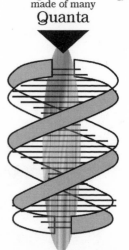

stored as information. The nervous system is how our brain and body communicate.

All the cells in the nervous system communicate with each other through an electro-chemical transmission, generally thought to occur through external stimulation. However, stimulation can occur from within the cell itself, originating in the nucleus of each neuron cell where the DNA molecule resides.

We know that the DNA molecule holds all the information to recreate the exact structure of the human body. Within the double helical DNA molecule, there is a greater potential of information than we had ever thought possible, characterized as a pulsating current made up of quanta, or bundles of energy.

Each quantum in the pulsating current is not just a bundle of energy, but it is a bit of information specific to the place and time from which it originated, and it holds the evolution-ary information about all life on the planet.

The pulsating quanta current has the capacity to affect the intra-cellular environ-

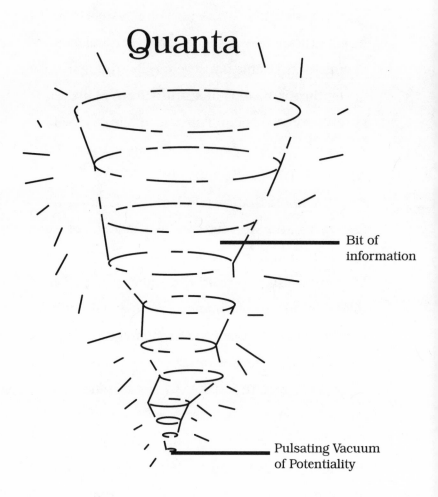

Quanta

Bit of
information

Pulsating Vacuum
of Potentiality

ment by either extenuating or inhibiting the stimulation of the neuron cell. Much like the external stimulation of a neuron cell, the internal stimulation of a neuron cell provides us with self-experiences within our body.

Therefore, at the deepest level of quantum nervous system functioning, matter equals quantum energy, and quantum energy equals bits of information.

Each individual quantum in the pulsating DNA current is an infinitely small vortex of energy similar to a tornado. Each vortex of quantum energy is said to have a vibratory frequency (a motion of moving back and forth) and a wave-like oscillation (a motion of moving up and down). The interaction of the vibratory frequency and wave-like oscillation of each quantum is exactly one bit of information.

There is a hidden quantum variable at the apex, or smallest point of the spinning tornado-like vortex of every quantum, referred to as the Pulsating Vacuum of Potentiality.

The Universal Heartbeat connects all information throughout all time and space, and is the binding integrity of all quanta and all information that quanta represent.

The pulsation of the vacuum is an undulating motion of infinite velocity, and this is common in all quanta everywhere, happening at the same time and rate, and can be described as a Universal Heartbeat. This Universal Heartbeat connects all information throughout all time and space; it is the binding integrity of all quanta and all information that quanta represent.

If we look at this theory as a model to understand our experience in day-to-day life, we can see that information is stored in the body in various places: from the brain to nerve cells to DNA and quanta. All of this information is experienced daily through our nervous system.

If we consider this as one visual and conditional interpretation of a universal truth, we can see how information is not just specific to each quanta, but to each human being, to each village, town, city, country, planet, solar system, and galaxy. In understanding the theory in this way, we can see it is a Universal Truth.

All of the information that makes up our infinitely vast and conditional universe is contained or embraced in Unconditional Love.

Universal Heartbeat

I would like to take Dr. Bonnici's study a step further and say that if the Pulsating Vacuum of Potentiality at the apex of every quantum binds all information throughout time and space, then any information in the quanta is a partial reflection of Unconditional Love.

Since Unconditional Love is all accepted information throughout time and space, before time and space, and beyond time and space, whether it is one bit or all quanta information, it is a part of the unlimited accepted information that is Unconditional Love.

Dr. Bonnici talks about the "Universal Heartbeat in the Vacuum of Potentiality." I look at the Universal Heartbeat in the Vacuum of Potentiality as the dynamic relationship between each individual quanta and Unconditional Love.

The Vacuum of Potentiality can be described as an infinite mirror. On one side, this

Our limited experience in the conditional world is overwhelmed by the reality of Unconditional Love. This feeling of being overwhelmed causes a resistance that is the felt friction in our bodies.

mirror reflects the infinite embrace of Unconditional Love; on the other side, it reflects each bit of information embraced in our quantum-conditioned world. In other words, the Universal Heartbeat in the Vacuum of Potentiality is a two-part relationship between Unconditional Love and our conditional world.

All the information that makes up our infinitely vast and conditional universe is contained or embraced in Unconditional Love. Because of the infinite magnitude of the information contained in Unconditional Love, our limited experience in the conditioned world is overwhelmed by the reality of Unconditional Love. This feeling of being overwhelmed causes a resistance that is the felt friction in our bodies. It is normal for us to experience Primordial Fear in our relationship to Unconditional Love.

The experience of embrace and resistance happens an infinite amount of times in each moment and is what creates the Universal Heartbeat.

The experience of embrace and resistance to Unconditional Love happens an infinite amount of times in each moment and is what creates the Universal Heartbeat.

When we accept the understanding of this Universal Heartbeat, we begin to find our balance between humility and dignity. We may rest in the humility that we will always be a small part of the information that is Unconditional Love. However, we will also rest in the dignity and nobility that Unconditional Love is precisely the deepest part of who we are.

Unconscious Mind

The unconscious mind is the part of the mind that houses all thoughts and impulses of which the individual is not conscious or aware but which still influence emotions and behavior. Parts of the unconscious mind can become conscious in any one moment and then unconscious the next. This can be demonstrated by recalling a memory in one moment and noticing, by the next moment, another thought has taken its place.

The unconscious mind is made up of layers. Some layers contain the memories we retrieve daily, some contain things about which we have forgotten, and there are some other layers of the unconscious mind one may not yet know even exist. Stored in these layers are our fear of survival, our past experiences we have accepted, our past experiences we have not accepted but still fear, information passed on through generations of our human experiences, unconscious bodily sensations, genetic information, neuro-quantum information, universal quantum information, and the unconditional unconscious.

Top layers of the unconscious mind are easy to recall, but they can be superceded by information that exists at deeper levels.

An example of unconscious memories superceding a conscious decision is a story of a grandmother who always cut off the end of a ham before cooking it. Her grandson watched her do this for years. When he was older and preparing a ham for the oven, a friend asked why he had cut off the end of the ham. The grandson was unsure and called his grandmother to find out why she had always done that. His grandmother said that the ham was too large to fit in her pan. The man's pan was large enough for a whole ham, but his unconscious conditioning superceded his conscious mind when he cut the end off the ham.

Some layers of the unconscious exist within the complex neuro-circuitry of our

We can see that thinking to understand, listen and communicate is not only limited by our memories of experiences and what we know or do not know, but also by what we have been conditioned to know or not know by past generations.

brain. This is where we do most of our thinking to understand, listen, and communicate in our day-to-day life. We can see that thinking to understand, listen, and communicate is not only limited by our memories of experiences and what we know or do not know, but also by what we have been conditioned to know or not know by past generations.

Just like our brain, the body stores information or memory in its cellular structure of muscles, bones, ligaments, organs, etc. For example, after four operations on my left knee, I have developed many cellular memories in my muscles, bones, and ligaments associated with the continual trauma to that area of my body. My knee still gets stiff and my right hip gets sore from overcompensating. These cellular memories were created to protect my knee from the traumatic accidents and operations it had experienced.

There are ways to work with the body to help it accept and release these memories; but

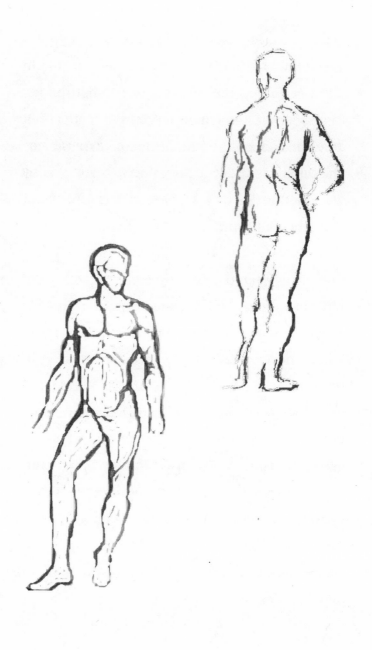

typically, the more intense the experience, the harder it is to release.

A layer of the unconscious mind in our genetic coding has made it possible for the body to develop into the human form. Deeper into the unconscious, we find information coded in the quanta that is specific to each of us from the place and time we originated and to all of our individual conditional experiences.

The next layer of the unconscious is at the apex of the quanta, where the relationship between a conditional and an unconditional existence is characterized as the Primordial Fear that lies within each of us. This is the unconscious Primordial Fear of an uncondi-tional existence that makes up the universal unconscious.

The final layer of our unconscious mind is the unconditional unconscious mind of Unconditional Love, which is so large, that when acknowledged, it can supercede all other layers of the unconscious.

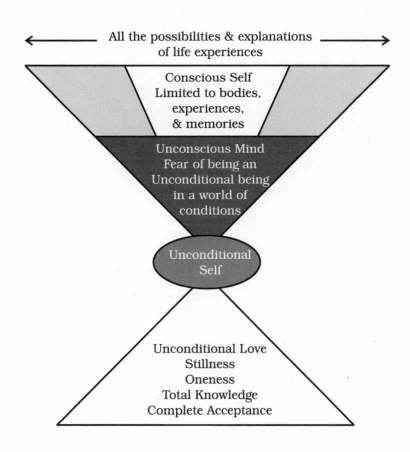

The deepest layer of the unconscious
mind in each human being is
Unconditional Love.

For example, when one faces death, one is looking directly at Unconditional Love. One either sees one's own Primordial Fear (expressed as all life experiences not yet accepted) or acknowledges that Unconditional Love is on the other side. Either way, this type of an experience can have a profound effect on the way one expresses oneself to the world, even if for a moment.

All of these layers of the unconscious mind are in each of us, however, the deepest layer of the unconscious mind in each human being is Unconditional Love.

We can see that conditionally it may take many years and generations to work through all the layers of the unconscious mind to get to the understanding of Unconditional Love. However, if we look at all these layers of the unconscious mind as filtered expressions of a larger unconscious mind called Unconditional Love, we can understand our individual unconsciousness as filtered expressions of Unconditional Love and begin to see a way of

What keeps us from
seeing our individual
filtered expression
as a part of
Unconditional Love
is our lack of awareness
or fear of our own
Primordial Fear.

accepting all these layers as a part of where we are right now in life.

What keeps us from seeing our individual filtered expression as a part of Unconditional Love is our lack of awareness or fear of our own Primordial Fear.

Awareness of our own Primordial Fear can be achieved individually by unconditioning the body to completely accept or unconditionally love the unconscious part of our mind that is Primordial Fear. In doing this, we are allowing the body to physically experience the communication and relationship between that which is conditional and that which is Unconditional Love in any one moment of life.

Such unconditioning can also be achieved universally when the majority of human beings on our planet accept Primordial Fear as our relationship to Unconditional Love and part of our common conditional life. This means that the more people who accept this experiential validity, the less resistance the individual will

Unconditioning of our fear
of Primordial Fear can
be achieved universally
when the majority of
human beings on our
planet accept Primordial
Fear as our relationship
to Unconditional Love
and part of our common
conditional life.

If Primordial Fear
becomes completely
accepted or
unconditionally loved as
a part of a conditional
life, it is easier for us to
accept our fears and look
past them.

have accepting his/her relationship to Unconditional Love in his/her life and death.

Unconditionally accepting or loving our Primordial Fear as a part of life allows us to dissolve our fears of it and makes all levels of our unconscious more visible. Our resistance to our fears is what keeps us from seeing them as a part of who we are.

If Primordial Fear becomes completely accepted or unconditionally loved as a part of a conditional life, it is easier for us to accept our fears and look past them. Perhaps Franklin D. Roosevelt described it best when he said: "The only thing we have to fear is fear itself."

Fear of fear keeps us in bondage and our liberation lies within accepting it.

An individual or group expression reveals what we accept about life, what we fear about life, and the combination of these two is how we make life acceptable to ourselves.

Expression

Expression is the way that any individual or group behaves and acts within the world. Individual human expression is how one communicates to the world verbally, physically, emotionally, and psychologically; it is created by a combination of behaviors learned throughout one's life.

The shared expression of a group of people is manifested in their similar beliefs and perceptions about the world around them.

An individual or group expression reveals what we accept about life, what we fear about life, and the combination of these two is how we make life acceptable to ourselves.

Unconditional Acceptance of Individual Expression

Individual or group expressions are created by what we have accepted and what we have not accepted as a part of life. Individuals and groups label what they have accepted or not accepted according to language and culture. These individual and group expressions have the capacity to nourish the diversity of ways to live and be in the world. However, they can also manifest the detrimental capacity to exclude the understanding or acceptance of other expressions.

An optimum individual or group expression would minimize a sense of absolute exclusiveness while maximizing the shared experiential depth of all human beings and our individual relationship with Unconditional Love. The relationship, as it has been described, is our individual experience of our own Primordial Fear.

*In accepting our relationship
with Unconditional Love
as Primordial Fear,
we begin to see our own and others'
individual expressions more clearly,
and it becomes obvious
we all share the same
embodied human experience,
expressing it in different ways.*

If we are afraid of this relationship, we are unable to see past our own expression, thus believing our specific expression is the only way to have a relationship with Unconditional Love.

If we accept our relationship with Unconditional Love and our own Primordial Fear, we are able to see past our expression, which has been created by specific historical, cultural, and experiential factors. When we are able to see past our own expression, we see that others' expressions (also created by specific historical, cultural, and experiential factors) are simply the way they relate to their relationship with Unconditional Love or their own Primordial Fear. We begin to see our own and others' individual expressions more clearly; it becomes obvious that we all share the same embodied human experience, expressing it in different ways.

When our relationship with Unconditional Love and our own Primordial Fear is feared or not accepted, it causes suffering commonly

Knowing this relationship with Primordial Fear resides in our own unconscious is what makes us conditionally connected in an unconditional way.

expressed as fear of death, old age, illness, loss, the need to feel connected, and/or the need to feel separate and in control. When this relationship with Unconditional Love or our own Primordial Fear is accepted, it is commonly expressed as love, joy, happiness, inspiration, and excitement.

It is easier to recognize our relationship to Unconditional Love or our own Primordial Fear in everyday life when we begin to look at some of these commonly known experiences, not only in our own life, but in others' as well. We begin to see we all have a combination of fear and acceptance of this relationship to Unconditional Love that makes up our individual expressions.

It is our individual relationship with Unconditional Love that makes us each unique. Knowing this relationship with Primordial Fear resides in our own unconscious is what makes us conditionally connected in an unconditional way.

*Individually working
to allow the body to accept the
unconditional relationship
known as Primordial Fear is
an ongoing practice of accepting
that we are all a part of the same
Unconditional existence.*

Accepting the Unconditional Relationship Known as Primordial Fear

Individually working to allow the body to accept the unconditional relationship known as Primordial Fear is an ongoing practice of accepting that we are all a part of the same Unconditional existence. This can be difficult because we each are attached to our individual conditional expression, and the degree of attachment is equal to the degree of our resistance to consciously experience and accept our own Primordial Fear.

Thus, the challenge for each of us is to soften our hold on what we know, to accept our fundamental not-knowing, and to ease control of our individual world and our relationships. If we accept this challenge, we liberate ourselves from the fear compelling us

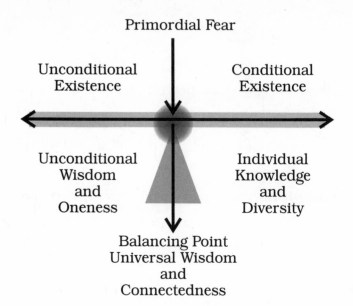

Primordial Fear

Unconditional Existence

Conditional Existence

Unconditional Wisdom and Oneness

Individual Knowledge and Diversity

Balancing Point Universal Wisdom and Connectedness

to uphold our conditional expression and its tenuous sense of embodied confidence, and we can finally rest in the deep confidence that naturally arises from our relationship with Unconditional Love. That fear is then freed to realize itself in the experiences of gratitude, joy, compassion, and creativity.

Accepting the call to our relationship to Unconditional Love or our own Primordial Fear can be seen as a point of balance where we can maintain individuality and clearly see our connectedness to everything around ourselves. This point of balance is not static, but it is rather a dynamic interplay of daily life and relationships that becomes evident when we realize our own felt experience is a continual acknowledgement of the humility and dignity of who we really are.

Through practice of this balance, the experience of being human becomes an ever-deepening understanding of ourselves and our relationship to Unconditional Love.

*Humility arises from the
understanding that fear
is part of a conditional
world and we only have the
capability to minimize it,
not to get rid of it.*

*Dignity arises from the
understanding that at the
base of all fear is our own
Primordial Fear
or our relationship with
Unconditional Love.*

Humility arises from the understanding that fear is part of a conditional world and we only have the capability to minimize it, not to get rid of it. Dignity arises from the understanding that at the base of all fear is our own Primordial Fear or our relationship with Unconditional Love.

This understanding lets us know that each of us is a part of the vast integrity, compassion, and wisdom that is Unconditional Love.

If we understand that all of our individual expressions arise from Primordial Fear, we can become united through our common embodied experience of humility and dignity.

Unity Through Common Fear

If we understand that all of our individual expressions arise from Primordial Fear, we can become united through our common embodied experience of humility and dignity. Throughout human history, facing a common fear has always brought people together. From natural disasters to war, people have stood together beyond their differing beliefs to help each other through a common fear.

In an effort to work at accepting or denying an event that creates fear on such a massive social scale, most individuals unite with the majority of people who respond to the fear in a similar way. Often this results in feelings of great unity, empathy, and compassionate acts toward others who respond in the same way.

By understanding Primordial Fear as a common denominator for embodied human existence, we can rise above all the personal,

*If the majority of humans
understand and accept
this Primordial Fear
as the fear from which
every other fear arises,
it can bring us closer
together as a race.*

racial, religious, and cultural fears that keep us apart. It can bring us together in an empathetic and compassionate way because we are experiencing and trying to accept an embodied Fear common to us all.

If the majority of humans understand and accept this Primordial Fear as the fear from which every other fear arises, it can bring us closer together as a race.

The Embodied
Daily Life
Practice of
Unconditional
Love

Processing Information
with the Intuitive Body
and/or
the Thinking Mind

In everyday life, we use our thinking mind to process our moment-to-moment experience, which can hinder our ability to understand an experience or enhance it. We can sense when our thinking mind is hindering or enhancing our immediate experience through an awareness of our body's feedback system of tension and ease.

Because our thinking mind is processing information through experiences we have accepted and through experiences we have not accepted and still fear, the processing capability of the thinking mind is limited to the experiences we have had in our lifetime. It is limited in its capacity to process information with clarity and insight due to dysfunctional patterns of thought that are conditioned by these past experiences.

These dysfunctional thought patterns continue to unconsciously influence the processing of our thinking mind and daily behavior. However, if we become conscious that these dysfunctional patterns exist, then we have the opportunity to practice accepting the experience from which they emerged.

Conditioned patterns of thought and behaviors that were conscious and functional in the past may have become dysfunctional and unconscious in the present. For example, a child might fling herself on the ground and throw a tantrum if she does not get what she wants. This form of behavior does not work well for adults, so most of us have found other ways to ask for things. Some patterns of existence that we used as children or young adults had a function at that time, but as we got older, these same patterns became a dysfunctional part of our unconscious mind.

Although the mind is limited in its ability to process the information of felt experience, our body's innate wisdom is capable of intuitively processing information in a more original and organic way.

Although the mind is limited in its ability to process the information of felt experience, our body's innate wisdom is capable of intuitively processing information in a more original and organic way. A good example of this is the way we are able to intuitively process information in the early stages of life. As children, we were able to intuitively process a vast amount of felt information before we began to use our thinking mind. This bodily processing of information was not hindered by fears of unaccepted past experiences.

For example, children exposed to a variety of languages at a young age can learn them more easily because they are less conditioned to any one way of expression shared through social interaction. They are more open to accepting different ways of expressing themselves without the fear of not understanding these different expressions. In adulthood, these accumulated fears are usually experienced as self-judgment, defensiveness, withdrawal, anxiety, stress, depression, etc.

*Recovering our body's capacity
to intuitively process information
without the hindrances of
self-judgment, conditioned patterns
of thought, and other reactive
limitations of our thinking mind,
liberates us to use that same
thinking mind in complimentary
relationship with the felt innate
wisdom arising in our
intuitive body.*

Recovering our body's capacity to intuitively process information without the hindrances of self-judgment, conditioned patterns of thought, and other reactive limitations of our thinking mind liberates us to use that same thinking mind in complimentary relationship with the felt innate wisdom arising in our intuitive body.

Practicing trusting the intuitive body to process information can be difficult because the thinking mind has conditioned itself not to trust the intuitive body. This mistrust occurs when the thinking mind cannot integrate, process, or accept all the felt experiences arising in the body. This mistrust is fundamentally a condition of fear and the thinking mind's creation of distance or a separation between itself and the intuitive body.

The more the thinking mind continues to not accept an experience, the more it conditions the body to fear. This, in turn, restricts the intuitive body's wisdom from its open and spontaneous expression.

When we completely experience our self as the intuitive body we realize our unconditional self.

In order to allow the intuitive body to process the fear of our thinking mind, we have to relax our dominant identification with our thinking mind and its mistrust of the body. When we completely experience our self as the intuitive body, we realize our unconditional self. Our intuitive body is exactly our unconditional self.

The experience of our unconditional self is fundamentally a felt experience of integrated wholeness and sensorial awareness without words or thoughts. From this awareness of our unconditional self, we can compassionately view the conditioned and reactive thought patterns of our thinking mind as a physical sensation of fear in our body.

The practice of having a compassionate embodied awareness and accepting the arising sensations of fear in our body is a constant process of relaxing our culturally and personally conditioned identification with our thinking mind. Such relaxing has the tendency to arouse a variety of personal and mundane fears

*The experience
of our unconditional self
is fundamentally a felt experience
of integrated wholeness and
sensorial awareness
without words or thoughts.*

in our body, and begins to reveal an embodied depth of Primordial Fear common to all human beings.

Our thinking mind is not usually conscious of Primordial Fear, but Primordial Fear is a constantly felt reality in the organic structure of our body. Being intimately conscious of our moment-to-moment sensation of Primordial Fear, we come to realize it as our relationship to the infinite information potential of Unconditional Love.

*The felt bodily experience of
our unconditional existence
is a preverbal, yet conscious,
realization that we are never
removed from the integrated
wholeness and infinite
information that pervades
all life and death.*

Meeting and Understanding the Felt Experience of Primordial Fear in the Body

The experience of Primordial Fear is the felt friction experienced in our conditional body when it becomes consciously aware of its intimacy with an unconditional existence, and it is common to all human beings regardless of race, culture, or creed.

More specifically, the felt bodily experience of our unconditional existence is a pre-verbal, yet conscious, realization that we are never removed from the integrated wholeness and infinite information that pervades all life and death. This unconditional grace of our beginning-less and endless intimacy with all information is the experience of Unconditional Love.

Unconditional Love is exactly the experience of always being embraced just as we are.

Unconditional Love
is exactly the experience
of always being
embraced just as we are.

Initial Exercise for Experiencing Primordial Fear in the Body

You can feel your intimate relationship to Primordial Fear by taking two to five minutes to do the following exercise:

Find a comfortable place to lie down, preferably on your bed, a mat, or some carpeted area.

Lie down with your arms at your side and your feet naturally falling away from each other.

Then close your eyes and begin to slow your breathing. Let your body begin to yield and sink with the pull of gravity.

Allow all your muscles, organs, bones, and joints to relax and melt into the surface on which you are lying. Start with visualizing your toes melting and then move to your ankles, shins, thighs, stomach, chest, neck, face, shoulders, arms, and hands.

When you feel completely relaxed and at ease in your body, slowly open your eyes and

Recover the trust in your body's ability to accept the felt intimacy with Unconditional Love.

notice the felt sensation that moves through
your entire body.

Feel how, moments later, it dissipates.

This momentary bodily sensation is the
inner friction or Primordial Fear that arises
from your body's felt awareness of its relationship to Unconditional Love. It is momentary
and fleeting because, as an individual, your
thinking mind and your conditioned identity
are not able to immediately process, integrate,
or accept all the felt information arising in the
experience of Primordial Fear. That information is not only the felt awareness of your
intimate relationship with Unconditional Love,
but is also the realization of your original or
unconditional identity.

The significance of this initial exercise
is to begin to recover the trust in your body's
ability to accept the felt intimacy with Unconditional Love, and to relax your attachment to
your thinking mind and conditioned identity
as an individual.

When you take the time to do this exercise
daily, you are in fact acknowledging the impor-

*Acknowledging the importance
of your relationship to
Unconditional Love will deepen
the felt bodily awareness of your
unconditional existence.*

tance of your relationship to Unconditional Love and are sincerely demonstrating your willingness to deepen the felt bodily awareness of your unconditional existence.

This exercise gives you a way to consciously relax your body, provides a tangible sensation you can physically recall, and introduces you to the body's way of processing information.

The fight / flight instinct is fundamentally a reaction to the body's felt experience of fear.

Relaxing the Fight / Flight Instinct with Unconditional Breathing

Once you have initiated your felt bodily relationship to Unconditional Love, you can continue to deepen that relationship through the practice of breathing.

As infants, our breathing was natural or unconditioned. We breathed instinctively through our nostrils and into our lower abdomen. As we grew older, we experienced many situations that we did not understand or accept, which initiated a primitive behavior in the body called the fight / flight instinct. This fight / flight instinct is fundamentally a reaction to the body's felt experience of fear and causes us to defensively tighten the lower abdomen and breathe rapidly and shallowly into our upper chest.

*The thinking mind's inability
to understand an experience only
reinforces the experience of fear
and keeps us in a constant
cycle of mistrust and fear.*

When breathing into the chest, we are, in fact, mistrusting the body and not allowing it to process the uncomfortable feelings arising from fear often experienced in the heart region. Such mistrust localizes awareness in the thinking mind. The thinking mind's inability to understand the experience only reinforces the experience of fear and keeps us in a constant cycle of mistrust and fear.

Consciously reminding the body of the unconditioned state of breathing into the lower abdomen can help put awareness back into the body.

In general, we focus most of our awareness in our heads, thinking about our felt experiences and trying to understand them. When we localize our awareness in the process of our thinking mind, we tend to diminish our inner felt bodily awareness and distance ourselves from our immediate sensory experience.

Because our awareness spends so much time remembering and processing our life experience through our thinking mind, we

The practice of breathing
past the chest
and
into
the
lower abdomen
can help begin a more
trusting awareness
in the body.

constantly condition ourselves to the illusion that our memories and thinking mind are all that we are.

The practice of breathing past the chest and into the lower abdomen can help begin a more trusting awareness in the body, thereby allowing the mind to have a chance at relaxing with the idea of its awareness of being a part of a conditional experience it does not completely understand. It also allows our embodied awareness to differentiate itself from personal memories and thoughts of the thinking mind to understand that unconditionally we are so much more than just our thinking mind.

The Practice of Unconditional Breathing

Exercise 1

Begin the practice of unconditional breathing by lying down with your eyes closed, with your arms at your side, and your feet naturally falling away from each other.

Visualize your breath as you inhale through your nose, following it all the way to your abdomen, two to three inches below your belly button.

Allow your stomach to fill up like a balloon. Let yourself experience the pause at the end of the inhalation.

Then let your belly collapse naturally and follow your breath up your chest, through the throat, and out your nose. Once again, let yourself experience the pause at the end of the exhalation.

After you have practiced this abdominal breathing for two to five minutes and experienced the pause at the end of the inhalation and exhalation, slowly begin to open your eyes. As in the initial exercise above, be aware of any sensation in your body when opening your eyes.

Practice this abdominal breathing and the felt experience when opening your eyes, two to five minutes a day for a week, to start unconditioning the body from its reactive fight / flight instinct.

Exercise 2

After at least a week of practicing abdominal breathing with your eyes closed, begin to practice the same exercise with your eyes open.

Remember to keep your arms at your side and your feet naturally falling away from each other.

Just let yourself gaze softly at the ceiling.

Do this abdominal breathing with your eyes open for two to five minutes a day for a week.

Exercise 3

After following two to three weeks of practicing abdominal breathing in a lying position, you can begin to work with the same breathing technique in a seated position.

Eyes gazing softly,
breathe into your lower abdomen.

Practice the seated position either on a chair or on a pillow on the floor.

As in the lying-down position, keep your eyes softly opened at a forty-five degree angle and remain wakeful to the sensation of your abdominal breathing.

Try to keep your spine in a natural, upright posture without creating any tension in your back or shoulders.

Practice this seated position for two to five minutes a day, preferably in the morning.

Exercise 4

After your body becomes familiar with abdominal breathing in the lying down and seated positions with eyes open, you can begin to extend your practice to include other positions like standing and walking. This is the beginning of integrating abdominal breathing and grounding yourself in your body during daily life.

Practice being aware of your abdominal breathing while walking to your car, sitting at

*Integrate abdominal breathing
into your daily life.*

your desk, working at your job, waiting in a grocery line, doing the dishes, or changing a diaper. This technique is done with your eyes open, and it can be practiced anywhere.

It is simple enough for anyone to practice three to five breathing cycles here and there throughout the day. Although you practice abdominal breathing throughout the day, *do not neglect your lying down or seated practice.*

Simultaneous training of your home practice and your daily life activities are necessary to continually uncondition your body into abdominal breathing, relaxation, and alert wakefulness. Simultaneous practice will prevent your body from reverting back to shallow breathing and reactivity of your fight / flight instinct.

This practice is similar to making the decision to change your eating habits. It is not about practicing a strict diet for a specific period of time, but it's about changing your

*Your abdominal breathing
is not just a temporary
practice, but becomes a
means of healthy living as
a way of life.*

eating habits as a way of life. Your abdominal breathing is not just a temporary practice, but it becomes a means of healthy living as a way of life.

Beginning Your Felt Relationship to Information in Your Body

After a month of practicing Exercises 1 through 4, begin the practice of becoming intimate with sensations that are happening in your body by deepening your practice of abdominal breathing in a seated position.

Take your seated position as usual, making sure you sit upright but in a comfortable and relaxed way.

Keep your eyes softly opened, thinking of them as mirrors, allowing them to rest at a forty-five degree angle.

Begin your inhalation following the breath through your nose, down your throat, and guide it gently to your lower abdomen. At the pause of the inhalation, rest your felt awareness of being in your lower abdomen.

At the natural end of the pause, let your belly collapse and follow the air with your awareness as is rises up your chest, throat, and out your nostrils. At the end of the exhalation, be aware of the pause.

Do this cycle of inhalation and exhalation until you have a sense of relaxation and presence in your body.

Once you have achieved a relaxed presence in your body and a felt sense of being in the lower abdomen, begin extending your awareness to sensations in your body.

Take your inhalation in the manner described above, continue to rest your awareness at the pause and with the sense of being in your lower abdomen.

As your exhalation naturally begins from your lower abdomen, follow the air as it goes up through your chest and become aware of any felt sensations in the area of your heart. Do not hold on to or linger in any sensation that you may be feeling in your chest or heart area, just continue to follow the air as it leaves your nostrils. Again, become aware of the pause at the end of the exhalation.

Effortlessly, begin your next inhalation, following the air through your nostrils, past your chest, and into your abdomen. At the end of the inhalation, remember to allow yourself to rest in the felt sense of being in your lower abdomen during the natural pause.

Continue to allow your belly to naturally collapse following your exhalation and become aware of any felt sensation. Again, not lingering in the sensation, let your awareness follow the air as it leaves your nostrils.

Continue this cycle of breathing for two to five minutes a day, preferably in the morning.

Note: Sensations in the chest or heart area may have a felt quality of denseness, heaviness, tightness, a small quivering, lightness, spaciousness, and openness.

*Become familiar with the
sensations in your chest
or heart area and realize
they are felt information
the body is processing.*

Practicing Being
in the Whole Body

O nce you become familiar with the sensations in your chest or heart area, you will become aware they are, in fact, felt information the body is processing.

Your body processes this felt information in three ways, the first being physically containing or grasping experiences we hold in our body because we fear losing them. Some feelings associated with containing or grasping are anxiety, denseness, quivering, and tightness.

The second way our body processes felt information is physically protecting ourselves from experiences by pushing away feelings because of the fear of losing control or being overwhelmed. Some feelings associated with pushing away can include tightness, anxiety, defensiveness, a closed feeling, and numbness.

*Giving the whole body a chance
to process felt information helps
us completely accept, rather than
succumb, to our reactive tendencies
of grasping and pushing away.*

These first two ways of holding on to or pushing away felt information in the body are both resistance to a conscious relationship with Unconditional Love felt as Primordial Fear. This felt experience of holding on or pushing away is actually our fear of Primordial Fear itself.

The third way the body processes information arising out of our felt experience is through a process of bodily acceptance which begins by easing our tendency toward grasping and pushing away. As we allow our body to process the felt sensation in our chest, we release ourselves to experience those sensations throughout our whole body. Thus, the bodily feeling of acceptance is not localized in our chest but actually opens up into our whole body. Giving the whole body a chance to process this felt information helps us completely accept, rather than succumb, to our reactive tendencies of grasping and pushing away.

Once we have a felt understanding or complete acceptance of the experience in our

*Once we have a felt understanding
or complete acceptance of the
experience in our body, we have
the opportunity to respond with
compassion and wisdom for the
mutual benefit of ourselves
and others.*

body, we have the opportunity to respond with compassion and wisdom for the mutual benefit of ourselves and others. Feelings associated with acceptance are lightness, spaciousness, openness, gratitude, excitement, inspiration, and joy.

Exercise for Being in the Whole Body

Now we will practice a breathing technique that will expand your body's ability to move through and accept the felt information arising out of your immediate experience. Start by practicing this breathing technique in your seated practice and then integrate it into your daily life practice.

Begin your inhalation, following your breath through your nose, down your throat, and guide it gently to your lower abdomen. At the pause of the inhalation, rest your felt awareness of being in your lower abdomen.

At the natural end of the pause, let your belly collapse and follow the air with your awareness as it rises up your chest, throat, and out your nostrils. At the end of the exhalation, be aware of the pause.

Do this cycle of inhalation and exhalation until you have a sense of relaxation and presence in your body.

Once relaxed and present with a felt sense of being in the lower abdomen, again extend your awareness of sensations in your body.

Taking your inhalation in the manner described above, begin to rest your awareness at the pause and the sense of being in your lower abdomen.

As your exhalation naturally begins from your lower abdomen, follow the air as it goes up through your chest, becoming aware of, yet not holding on to or lingering in any felt sensations in the area of your heart. At this point of awareness in your heart area, recall the physical sensation of your Primordial Fear or your relationship with Unconditional Love.

As you remember, this felt sensation was experienced in the first phase of your lying-down practice when you went from closing your eyes to opening them.

Once you merge the sensation in your heart or chest with the felt recollection of your relationship with Unconditional Love, allow it to expand throughout the whole body. As you feel the tingling sensation permeating your whole body, imagine that same felt sensation as it releases through the pores of your skin.

When you practice releasing the sensation from the heart or chest area throughout your whole body and out all your pores, you now encourage your body to process felt information from this experience.

While the body is processing felt information, the mind is constantly seeking to understand the experience in terms of words,

While the body is processing felt information, the mind is constantly seeking to understand the experience in terms of words, concepts and ideas, and this interferes with the body's natural ability and wisdom to process the experience before thought.

concepts, and ideas; it interferes with the body's natural ability and wisdom to process the experience before thought. This is why it is important to let go of passing thoughts without holding on to them or pushing them away.

Working with a dense sensation in the chest or heart area before the body is able to move through all the information can be an ongoing process that takes days, weeks, or months. Depending on what experience you are having and the amount of information you are processing at a particular time, you may have a certain degree of information in the chest or heart area that was not released or processed completely through the pores of your skin.

When you have this kind of residual information, it may be helpful to go back to the lying-down position. You can work with the residual information for two to five minutes a day: first with your eyes closed and then with your eyes opened. Once you feel that your body has processed the information sufficiently, you can go back to your seated practice.

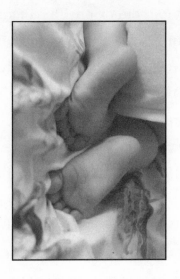

Be gentle with your body.

Be gentle with your body.

Realize that it may take time for it to accept or process certain experiences.

If you have some difficulty moving a dense sensation from your chest or heart throughout your whole body and the accompanying tingling sensation through to all your pores, again, it may be helpful to go back to your initial lying-down practice. Even if you may not initially experience the tingling sensation throughout the body or its release through your pores, continue to visualize, recall, and practice the processing of information without holding onto or pushing away any thoughts of self-judgment or self-criticism.

Your sincere practice of this exercise will help the body to recall and recover a child-like processing of felt information before thoughts and words. Young children are not as hindered or conditioned by self-criticism and self-judgment, which is why they are able to learn and process information through their body so

*Children experience life
with the whole body.*

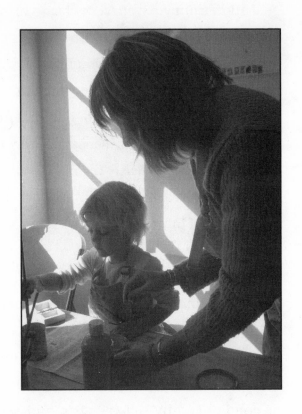

*Young child-like processing
is not as hindered or conditioned
by self-criticism and self-judgment.*

quickly. Children experience life with the whole body, whereas adults consume large amounts of energy to understand felt experience with only the thinking mind.

By making it a priority to give the body a chance to process information prior to the thinking mind, we are able to conserve energy and more efficiently process the passing flow of felt experience.

Practicing a
Moment-to-Moment
Relationship
with Unconditional Love

The exercise of being grounded in your whole body, while processing felt information, can be practiced anywhere at any time with awareness and self-compassion. You get a sensation of connectedness and compassionate understanding that needs no explanation in words, but needs only be experienced and felt in your body throughout your day-to-day life.

Consciously applying this phase of your practice in your daily mundane routines is easiest and good practice. However, this phase of practice is most effective in application to daily experiences that are out of the ordinary, such as when someone yells at you, when you are startled by a car horn or cut off in traffic, when you witness a gorgeous sunset, when a rainbow surprises you with its intensity and beauty, or when you feel excitement meeting someone to whom you are emotionally and/or sensually attracted. All of these experiences can give you an opportunity to practice unconditional love and respond in a manner that is compassionate, wise, meaningful, and more in line with who you really are.

When someone yells at you, it is helpful to stay grounded in your body and allow the felt sensations to pass through you so that you can freely respond in a way that is non-reactive and can diffuse the situation.

If you do not stay grounded in your body and allow the felt sensations to pass through, but instead tighten up and defensively protect yourself from feeling, you increase your reactive tendency to lash out verbally or behaviorally. This brings the detrimental impact and negative intensity of the experience beyond what is necessary for yourself and the other.

Let the more difficult times
flow through the body
to the ever-deepening
ocean of Unconditional Love
where you are completely embraced.

The capacity to be grounded in your body with self-compassion and openness allows deepening of your intimacy with the wisdom arising in the felt relationship with Unconditional Love.

When anger and hatred are being verbally directed at you, let it flow through the body to the ever deepening ocean of Unconditional Love where you are embraced completely just as you are.

Many of us have seen a wondrous sunset that left us awestruck with felt bodily sensations of gratitude, intense appreciation, mysterious interconnectedness, and a deep sense of joy. During such life experiences, no matter how brief or spacious in time, we can receive the full impact of the felt sensation arising within our body. The tendency is for people to shut down the full intensity of the experience by describing it with their thinking mind, thus protecting themselves from pleasurable experiences by labeling, categorizing, and/or explaining them.

*We can realize the farthest reaches
of our felt human experiences of joy,
wonder, awe, mystery and oneness,
and enjoy a deeper intimacy
in our relationship with
Unconditional Love.*

We get overwhelmed with the felt meaning of vast amounts of information arising in our body during an experience of intense awe and wonder, which is actually the fear of losing our sense of self-identity, control, and personal knowing.

If we allow the magnitude of the arising feelings and sensations in our body to flow through us without interference from our thinking mind, we can realize the farthest reaches of our felt human experiences of joy, wonder, awe, mystery, and oneness, to enjoy a deeper intimacy in our relationship with Unconditional Love.

As clear communication with Unconditional Love becomes a normal practice, this intimacy will deepen further, and you will begin to realize everything in life is a potential source of felt information from Unconditional Love, helping you to respond with more wisdom, integrity, and compassion to relationships and daily situations.

Process information from Unconditional Love by allowing the felt information in your body to flow freely with acceptance.

When integrating the practice of processing felt information from Unconditional Love, begin by emphasizing the practice of being in your whole body. This means that you can practice moving throughout your day, breathing into your lower abdomen and allowing the felt information in your body to flow freely with acceptance.

*Being the unconditional body is
fully experiencing the sensations in
each moment of your life.*

Being the
Unconditional Body

Being the unconditional body is fully experiencing the sensations in each moment of your life.

When you practice abdominal breathing and allow your body to experience the tingling sensation throughout its pores, you are processing information from Unconditional Love. After training your body to breathe into the lower abdomen with every experience, it will naturally begin to breathe abdominally and center there without conscious effort.

You will feel naturally centered, thereby freely experiencing the arising sensations as they move throughout the body. You will spend less time focusing on breathing and more time experiencing information from Unconditional Love, and will begin to experience each moment with a sense of empowerment, courage, compassion, insight, and connectedness.

*Experiences that impact our
body in the present moment
will bring up felt sensations
of fear from unaccepted
experiences in our past.*

Being the unconditional body is not an absolute condition or a one-time achievement. Being the unconditional body does not mean that you will never experience anxiety, fear, or uncertainty. It does mean you are willing to practice your life experiences with a commitment to embody wakefulness, self-compassion, integrity, openness, and Unconditional Love.

Some experiences that impact our body in the present moment will bring up felt sensations of fear from unaccepted experiences in our past. When such fears arise, the thinking mind reactively associates the fear with some stimulus in the present moment. If you gently relax and detach from the thinking mind, the light of awareness turns back to your felt bodily experience with courage, self-honesty, and self-compassion.

In doing this, you allow the body to process the information and find it is a familiar past fear and that, at the core of felt experience, all fears are fears of Primordial Fear itself. It is the fear of recognizing and accepting your innate

*Being the unconditional body
is having a compassionate
understanding of the
relationship between our
unconditional existence and
our conditioned existence.*

relationship to Unconditional Love, the fear of a conditional being recognizing and accepting his or her unconditional nature or unconditional existence.

Being the unconditional body is having a compassionate understanding of this relationship between our unconditional existence and our conditioned existence.

As embodied beings, we experience many fears during our lifetime. Sometimes the body may experience more information than the thinking mind can process or handle; however, if you remember that felt information is just fear moving through the body, then you can relax the urgency to explain or understand it with your thinking mind. It is only in our fear of not being able to accept our felt experience that we are driven to explain it to ourselves and others.

When we are being the unconditional body, it is also understood that the balance between body processing and thought processing is necessary since both are valid ways of

*We must remember that the urgency
to analyze, categorize or label our
experience is always based
on the anxiety of meeting
Primordial Fear itself.*

processing our felt experience. Rather than relying on one to the exclusion of the other, we should practice an openness to the wisdom inherent in their unique but complementary ways of processing felt experience.

A way to work on this complementary relationship between the mind and the body is by not being so quick to analyze or categorize our felt experience, but rather to create a spaciousness inside ourselves for their dual presence to be acknowledged and trusted. This allows the body's organic wisdom to rise into our moment-to-moment consciousness.

We must remember that the urgency to analyze, categorize, or label our experience is always based on the anxiety of meeting Primordial Fear itself.

To relax this urgency, start noticing how your thinking mind initiates a sequence of word thoughts explaining the felt experience. Once you notice the sequence of word thoughts, practice letting go of your attachment to completing the explanation to yourself, an explanation you

*Allow your body to process
as much as possible
before your thinking mind.*

already know you could finish. By letting go, you become open to feeling the body processing information, thereby trusting your body's wisdom.

Return to your breath as a tool to bring your awareness back into your body and into the moment. Allow your body to process as much as it can before returning to your thinking mind. Realize that the urgency to think about the experience has diminished, and the mind is more open and clear in understanding. This practice can help you work toward being more aware of your unconditional body throughout your moment-to-moment life.

Listening, Healthy Communication, and Support

Listening, communicating, and supporting with the unconditional body are great ways to continue your practice.

The unconditional body realizes there are many ways to describe what we accept or fear about life. Our psychology, upbringing, and personal choices determine how we express our acceptance and fear to ourselves and others.

When listening to someone, instead of trying to word-think about what is being said, practice being in the whole body. Hear that person speak and ask yourself whether that person is talking about something s/he accepts or fears. Acknowledge whether you accept it or fear it. If what is being described is something you both accept, you will have a common understanding with that person. Your ability to relate will be easy. Share your common inter-

est, wonder, anticipation, excitement, inspiration, etc. Enjoy the variety of ways you both
may describe the same thing.

If someone describes something s/he
accepts but that you fear, be gentle with your
body and allow yourself to physically experience the fear as the person talks to you. Practice being in your body with the fear, staying
in the moment, away from your word-thinking
mind. Ask questions that will allow you more
time to process the information in the body
and release the information or fear around it.
Reveal a genuine willingness to understand
and simultaneously have compassion for
yourself, knowing that your body is processing
the fear of what is being said. Do this and you
will understand how to respond with growing
clarity toward the other person's experience.

If you react to the situation out of fear, do
not judge yourself or blame the other person.
Take a breath and realize that life will give you
more opportunities to work on it, until the fear
is accepted.

When someone describes something s/he fears and you accept, compassionately acknowledge and support the other person from understanding that you have your own fears. As that person's fear arises, you understand it as a physical embodiment of what s/he does not understand: an embodied question felt as a fear that may need help being answered.

One way that you can help someone answer his or her question or process his or her fear is to create a spaciousness and acceptance of the fear, sitting together in silence. Another way to help someone is to encourage him or her to talk while you listen with a compassionate and accepting ear. If you choose to help by describing your way of accepting the fear, be aware there are many ways to accept fears. The answer you share may become one of many explanations that will eventually help the person realize his or her own answer.

There is no right or wrong way for someone to come to accept fear.

If someone has too much fear about something, he or she may need space or time to work on it before accepting the fear enough to talk about it.

If someone is describing a fear that you also have, it is easy to relate to that person because you are feeling the same thing. Empathetic listening and honest dialogue can give you both the opportunity to accept the common fear you are both experiencing. Listen with the whole body and acknowledge that you both are working on the same fear. You may also want to sit together, supporting each other in silence, giving the space for each of you to physically work with it.

If one of you accepts the fear during the time you are sharing together, you can switch to one of the interpersonal formats above. For example, the one who accepts it can help the other answer his/her own question and come to accept the fear through compassionate listening and unconditional caring.

If you both continue to fear it, do not judge yourself or the other person. Realize life will give you both the opportunity to work on it again, whether it is with each other or with someone else.

When you judge the way someone accepts his or her life, you are actually expressing the fear you have about accepting those parts of yourself as an unconditional being in a world of conditions.

When you acknowledge and compassionately accept the fear underneath your judgment, you create an opportunity to respond with understanding toward another person, which helps minimize the amount of fear and confusion in our world.

To Enjoy Life
and Heal Our World

People can work on accepting life and their own fears in many ways. The best way to share the unique way you accept life is by example.

When you judge the way someone accepts his or her life, you are actually expressing the fear you have about accepting those parts of yourself as an unconditional being in a world of conditions. This simply adds to the sum total of all the fear in the world, keeping us in bondage to greed, aggression, and ignorance.

When you acknowledge and compassionately accept the fear underneath your judgment, you create an opportunity to respond with understanding toward another person, which helps minimize the amount of fear and confusion in our world.

As each of us works toward minimizing the amount of fear in our personal world by

*The more we accept
our daily experience of
fear as fundamentally
our relationship with
Unconditional Love, the
closer we come to realizing
peace on earth.*

learning about quanta information and by practicing the exercises in this book, our felt experience and relationship to Unconditional Love becomes an everyday affair. We open up to a better understanding of ourselves.

The more we accept our daily experience of fear as fundamentally our relationship with Unconditional Love, the closer we come to realizing peace on earth.

If we accept that Primordial Fear is the way we experience Unconditional Love in our day-to-day life, we then begin to feel and sense how it moves through the body. As we deepen our felt understanding of how Primordial Fear is related to our experience of Unconditional Love, we learn how to transform the quality and texture of our feelings in ways that promote more joy, compassion, and wisdom in our world.

We transform anxiety and fear into passion, wonder, inspiration, anticipation, and excitement. This transformation allows us to move toward enjoying more of what life has to

*Living as unconditional beings
in a world of conditions
allows us to know we are doing
everything possible to create the
world we are meant to have.*

offer and expand our experience of gratitude, compassion, and creativity to live a more productive, joyful, and creative life.

Practicing moment-to-moment awareness, through our individual growing expressions and by living as unconditional beings in a world of conditions, allows us to know we are doing everything possible to create the world we are meant to have.

Definition of Terms

Being the unconditional body

Fully experiencing the sensations in each moment of life; having a compassionate understanding of the relationship between unconditional existence and conditioned existence.

Conditional existence

Opposite to the universal infinite presence of Unconditional Love.

Conditioned love

Accepting someone if certain conditions apply.

Dignity

The honorable quality resulting from understanding that at the base of all fear is our own Primordial Fear or our relationship with Unconditional Love, and that Unconditional Love is precisely the deepest part of who we are.

"Divine" love

Love that extends to include love of yourself, another, all others, and all creation.

Expression

How an individual or group communicates to the world verbally, physically, emotionally, and psychologically; created by a combination of behaviors learned throughout life.

Friction

A felt experience of opposites coming in contact with each other or fear.

"Good" love

Love that extends to include yourself.

"Great" love

Love that extends to include yourself and another.

Humility

The state or quality of being humble and understanding that fear is a part of a conditional world and we only have the capability to minimize fear, not get rid of it; the acceptance that we will always be a small part of the information that is Unconditional Love.

Individual truth

An experience felt by one being; also called relative truth.

Love

A felt experience of accepting, knowing, and understanding.

Opposites

Any conditional existence in contrast to the universal infinite presence of Unconditional Love.

Primordial Fear

A primitive, fundamental, and original fear created by the relationship of opposites or a conditional existence.

Psychoneuroquantum Theory

A quantum model of Nervous System Function developed by Andrew Shugyo Bonnici, Ph.D., in 1978.

Pulsating Vacuum of Potentiality

A hidden variable at the smallest point of the spinning tornado-like vortex of every quantum that contains the Universal Heartbeat.

Relative truth

An experience felt individually; also called individual truth.

Unconditional

Total or complete.

unconditional love

A felt experience of total or complete acceptance, total or complete understanding, and total or complete knowing.

Unconditional Love

All accepted information throughout time and space, and after time and space; an infinite wisdom that penetrates life and death and that is the wholeness and integrity of all creation.

Unconditional unconscious mind of Unconditional Love

That which, when acknowledged, supercedes all other layers of the unconscious.

Unconscious mind

The part of the mind that houses all thoughts and impulses of which the individual is not conscious or aware, but which still influence emotions and behavior; of which the deepest layer is Unconditional Love.

Universal Heartbeat

The pulsation, with an undulating motion of infinite velocity, of the Pulsating Vacuum of Potentiality, that is common to all quanta everywhere and happens at the same time and rate; the relationship between Unconditional Love and our Universe.

Universal truth

An experience felt by all human beings.

About the Author

Eric Bonnici's life journey has been the guide in his calling to understand Unconditional Love in a world of conditions. Eric was raised in a Judeo-Christian and Zen Buddhist household, and grew up studying various applications of spirituality.

His intense practice of the martial art, Judo, "the gentle way," his great love of physics and mathematics, and his experience in the traditional working world have all greatly contributed to his study of Unconditional Love.

Eric is currently a businessman and entrepreneur as well as a certified Qi Gong instructor and Applied Meditation trainer and counselor. He lives on the Big Island of Hawaii and is a loving husband, father, son, brother, and friend.